T0160784

HOU
WA

SE OF

ᴏꜰ

TER

HOUSE OF WATER

MATTHEW NIENOW

Alice James Books
Farmington, Maine

10 9 8 7 6 5 4 3 2 1

Alice James Books are published by Alice James Poetry Cooperative, Inc., an affiliate
of the University of Maine at Farmington.

Alice James Books
114 Prescott Street
Farmington, ME 04938
www.alicejamesbooks.org

Library of Congress Cataloging-in-Publication Data

Names: Nienow, Matthew, author.
Title: House of water / Matthew Nienow.
Description: Farmington, ME : Alice James Books, [2016]
Identifiers: LCCN 2016011687 (print) | LCCN 2016018429 (ebook) | ISBN
9781938584640 (softcover : acid-free paper) | ISBN 9781938584695 (eBook)
Subjects: | BISAC: FAMILY & RELATIONSHIPS / Parenting / Fatherhood. | POETRY
/ American / General.
Classification: LCC PS3614.I368 A6 2016 (print) | LCC PS3614.I368 (ebook) |
DDC 811/.6--dc23
LC record available at https://lccn.loc.gov/2016011687

Alice James Books gratefully acknowledges support from individual donors, private
foundations, the University of Maine at Farmington, and the National Endowment
for the Arts.

Cover Art: Werner Knaupp, www.wernerknaupp.de.
© 2016 Artists Rights Society (ARS), New York / VG Bild-Kunst, Bonn
"Westmännerinseln 11.11.2011"
Acryl auf Leinwand, 70 x 50 cm

CONTENTS

ACKNOWLEDGMENTS

My sincere thanks to all the editors who first gave my work a space in which to live and be read. Without your encouragements, this book would not be what it is.

The Adroit Journal:	"Making a Rabbet Plane in the Machine Shop on the Hill"
	"I Have No Empire"
	"In the Boatyard"
AGNI online:	"Backing Out"
	"Center of Effort"
Alaska Quarterly Review:	"Before the Boat Is a Boat"
Beloit Poetry Journal:	"And"
	"O Anchor"
Connotation Press:	"Ballast"
	"In the Shop, a True Edge Is Possible"
	"Ode to the Preacher Jig"
Crazyhorse:	"Adjustments"
	"I Am Not Building an Ark"
Fogged Clarity:	"You Want Me to Say It Pretty"
	"From the Middle of It"
Narrative:	"House of Water"
	"The Importance of Doing Nothing"
	"Self-Portrait with Hammer"
	"Reprise"
New England Review:	"It's the Boat That Haunts You"
	"Ode to the Slick"
	"I Wear the Work upon My Clothes"
New Madrid:	"Nocturne with Mysterious Leak"
The Paris-American:	"The Shipwright's Prayer"
Poetry:	"Ode to the Gain"
	"Ode to the Belt Sander & This Cocobolo Sapwood"
	"Ode to the Steam Box"
	"End Grain"
	"Bad Year Anthem"
	"In the Year of No Work"
Poetry Northwest:	"Wrecking"
The Rattling Wall:	"Song of Tomorrow"

Southwest Review: "The Handshake"

Terrain.org: "For the Next Task, I Turn from the Bench"

"Who Belongs"

"Opening the Shop"

"I Have a Canvas Work Tote Entirely Devoted"

"The Magazine"

"O Anchor" was reprinted in *Best New Poets 2012* (ed. Matthew Dickman, series ed. Jazzy Danziger, University of Virginia Press, 2012), and was featured on *Verse Daily* on January 2, 2013 and again on December 31, 2013 as a 2013 Favorite, and later reprinted on *The Far Field*, the online collection of former Washington State Poet Laureate, Kathleen *Flenniken.*

"For the Next Task, I Turn from the Bench" was featured on *Poetry Daily* on June 5, 2013.

"Ode to the Steam Box," "Ode to the Belt Sander & This Cocobolo Sapwood," and "O Anchor" were reprinted in *Poets on Growth: An Anthology of Poetry and Craft* (Math Paper Press, 2015) edited by Peter LaBerge and Talin Tahajian.

"Self-Portrait with Hammer" and "Reprise" were named finalists in *Narrative's* 2012 30 Below Contest.

"Nocturne with Mysterious Leak" appeared in the chapbook, *The End of the Folded Map* (Codhill Press, 2011).

This book would not exist if not for the generous, and sometimes fierce, encouragement from C. Dale Young. Seriously, C. Dale. I can't thank you enough for all that you give.

For teachers, from the beginning: Diane LeBlanc, Eliot Khalil Wilson, Linda Bierds, and Rick Kenney. For conference workshop leaders who pushed me in new ways: Carl Phillips, Marianne Boruch, and Yusef Komunyakaa.

Bread Loaf, you changed my life by giving me a real community of writers and allowing me to believe in myself.

Great thanks to readers of early versions of this book: Phillip B. Williams, Luke Johnson, Matthew Olzmann, and Todd Boss.

And for other friendships in writing and poetry—without you I would be a husk of my current self: Ossian Foley, Tomás Q. Morín, Natalie Diaz, James Arthur, Jamaal May, Tarfia Faizullah, Zachary Watterson, Ed Skoog, Natasha Deón, Javier Zamora, Meg Day, Matthew Kelsey, Svetlana Beggs, Ben Evans, Abe Streep, David J. Daniels, Jeremy Bass, Christopher Ross, Justin Boening, Malachi Black, Jennine Capó Crucet, Michael Wiegers,

Laura Vecsey, Shann Ray Ferch, Corey Van Landingham, Lisa Fay Coutley, Joshua Rivkin, Kevin Craft, Ross White, Carmiel Banasky, and a huge thank you to those friends I am inevitably failing to name here because my brain is full of poems.

Carey Salerno, how lucky I am to have landed in your careful hands. You are an amazing editor—thoughtful and supportive. I would have it no other way.

Thank you also to Alyssa Neptune and Julia Bouwsma for your careful attention to many important details.

Thank you to the Northwest School of Wooden Boatbuilding for giving me an invaluable education in craftsmanship—I learned as much about writing poems in your stead as I did in an MFA program.

Thank you to *Poetry* Magazine and the Poetry Foundation, the National Endowment for the Arts, Artist Trust, and the Elizabeth George Foundation for significant financial support in the making of these poems.

None of this would be worth doing without my amazing wife, Elie, who stood by me through the glory and the shit. Thank you also to our amazing boys, River and Paikea, here in this book and beyond the pages: my best teachers in life.

And, of course, who would I be if it were not for my forbearers? All my love to you, Mom and Dad.

What the river says, that is what I say.
—William Stafford

All truths wait in all things...
—Walt Whitman

THE SHIPWRIGHT'S PRAYER

O hammering body
made of the teeth of saws,

made of mallets turned
on the lathe,

o awl, o holy geometry
of the try square and perfectly

sharpened pencil, o jar of rust,
catacomb for the nail,

tap and die, o threaded vacancy
in the wood, cantankerous

plumb bob dangling from
the high shelf, o tidy opening

let into the case before
the lead is cast,

impurities sent out
in black smoke,

o on-switch and tripped
breaker, dim light for

bright work, fat bit
chucked up, featherboard

kept with C-clamp, rough stock
in a stack in the corner,

o fence lock and push stick,
o blade spinning in the machine—

send the news ahead of time;
I will listen for your every word.

WRECKING

///////////////////////

My first day on the job before the job
was ever mine, the boat, a ship actually, loomed
above me: the red bottom paint and white
topsides, the dissected bulwarks and bare
sponsons, swollen in the net of scaffolding
and jack stands, the improbable balance of it all—
but up the ladder I climbed with my
purchased swagger and accidental charm,
with which I gave each hand a tool
to wield against rot, and so took
to raising the short-handled sledge, all day
bringing it down upon the back
of the pry bar, sending checks through
the diminishing fir until I could raise
long strips of the fibrous wood and smell
that which had long ago forgotten about
air, locked away in the light and dark bands
of winter and summer growth, and careful
I was around the button-headed spikes, bigger
than a finger, which needed to be sprung
loose from the beams with the mad-science
help of the slide hammer, vice grips welded
to a rod along which a weight
would run, galloping against the widening
at the rod's end, and the force, felt all through
my body, would wake the nail and most
often free it from the wood, though
all the same I felt pounded into the dark
underside of the boat's hidden chambers,
torqued and split into the smallest version
of myself, whose quietness and steady progress
were the only disguise I knew in keeping

myself employed. I was the boatyard's clock,
each struck plank sounding along the hidden
timeline of a new, and already spent, life.

ADUSTMENTS

////////////////////////////

We take off the guard.
It only gets in the way.
The riving knife too.
What does it know,
holding its long finger
through newly sawn
wood? I'd like to believe
in the terrible beauty
of the table saw,
the splayed nubbins,
the raker teeth,
the table itself, cast
into being the murky
water above the beast
we walk toward
over and over, reaching
our long hands close
to the patient mouth;
we push against the fence,
against the movement
of the blade, we keep
ourselves close
to ourselves; the machine
has such a way
with us, a voice
we cannot forget,
the spindle bright
enough to want—

SELF-PORTRAIT WITH HAMMER

In the beginning, I struck my own finger with the hammer, watched it
happen in low light, watched the waffle grid divot into the flesh
between knuckles, saw the rust spring, a slit of red snaking from the hidden—

In the beginning, I kept working, felt the useless swell within me while I made do
with the lesser counterparts. I was writing my own name in the encyclopedia of work.

In the beginning, I thought I was the hammer, the knob of bone at the base
of my palm knocking things together.

In the usual ways, I knocked against my life and, not surprisingly, my life knocked
back.

We had a son who seemed very much the hammer. His bone teeth clamored
at the breast. He was new to me, but the pounding was older than any of us.

In the beginning, I thought I knew what a hammer was; I thought a hammer was the
grief of entering a world never fully made.

At first, the son wanted to know how it worked, how the wood made room for the
nail.

In the beginning, I couldn't have cared less about the nails, the way they bent or
sometimes stained the wood. I never suspected that I might become so thin.

In the new beginning, I caught the son as he curled out of the womb, his purple face
puckered at the work of being made,

pounded his backside until air swept into his lungs,
dipped him in water, and placed my swollen finger in his hand,
which immediately knew the shape of the hammer.

It didn't take long before the son realized the hammer was as good for wrecking as it was in keeping things together.

In the beginning, I imagined myself merely a rock, fit well to the palm, with a hunger for driving stakes and breaking weaker rock. Until I was the weaker rock.

I AM NOT BUILDING AN ARK

not out of salvaged wood a ship

for anything more than to see

its backbone its stacked timbers joined

its scarfs and tenons its carlins

its frames white oak its staves of cedar

its ballast keel and borrowed wind

it could go anywhere on any waters

but is not for saving what may

be drowned by the rage of what I do

not believe in

but this
                        these shapes the water

makes so easily a space for

OPENING THE SHOP

Swing wide the double doors in the dust rising dim

Unlock the heart you keep in the cabinet of your gnarled self

Unlatch each finger from its presupposed grip

No hammer is yet needed

No blade or waterstone skimmed with dark grains of yesterday's work

Only the light's steady buzz

And your eye's slow progress

As over planking it passes

As over frames and the stern sheets' long horseshoe

Each bronze nail puckered surely around the rove

Leave your haste behind you

More than a day's work is at stake

ODE TO THE BELT SANDER & THIS COCOBOLO SAPWOOD

The belt kicks on with a whir & the whir
licks the end grain of the off-cut with a hint

of hesitation. A small wind of ochre dust
sweeps off the belt before the belt comes back

to where it was. The whole rooms swells
with the scent of cinnamon & desire.

How imprecise the smell of desire.

The wood takes on a sheen, a gloss
the grain can live behind without worry

of being forgotten. A single knot blinks
out of the small block & becomes

the eye of a hummingbird, its beak
bending around the edge of the wood,

its song captured in the annular rings.
To think, this block was tossed in

with the scrap. That the bird
could have been lost. Or burned.

ODE TO THE STEAM BOX

With a match I became a man
who summoned diesel

from the yellow caverns
of a ten-gallon jug, called the flame

now hissing out the hose
at the small house of water, that

rusted drum from which travels
an excruciating wetness—this

is what makes the body
otherwise, what makes it

sing. To take that
which has decided on a shape

and bend, without breaking,
the lengthening fibers. To give

the straight thing curve.
To make of the tree a song

grown long in a linseed skin,
the slick hot strake waiting

to become parcel
of the round world again.

ODE TO THE GAIN

There's the paring chisel's purpose
in the steamed cedar strake, its long warp

laid strong against the bench,
whose pocked surface is the book

of what has already been made
or marred in learning's wake—& clamped

now in the jaws one is
waiting for its match, for the chisel to elaborate

the pencil's scribed hypothesis, under which
lies another path, & through a tilting eye

the curving bevel's made, the chisel rolling
back tight scrolls of thinnest grain & what bright

sleeves begin to fleece the floor; there is a lack
given to the wood, some short song cut loose

from the lignin's name, that a longer &
more buoyant melody be made.

IN THE SHOP, A TRUE EDGE IS POSSIBLE

there, where a dozen sets of blades wait to estimate
the wood's potential, that warm open grain
honey-toned in the white light as it emerges

from the planer, and 10,000 crescent shavings dance
atop the new planet of the plank, until, borne into
my hands, I crank down the cutterhead and feed

it again and again into this machine that makes,
as best as it knows how, a calibrated version
of the truth, which might be repeated to whomever asks

after the stock's dimensions, here, where the work is to make
from one body one body while a cloud rises,
thickening in the air, yellowing the light,

and a heap of shavings hush underfoot, above which,
laid across the length of two benches, glows
the beauty I covet, already betrothed to that idea, that

accuracy that lives beyond fact, somewhere between
the made and the living thing,
before it was ever worked.

BACKING OUT

There is a plane with a convex sole,
a small segment of a circle
much larger than the plane or any

piece of wood the plane might work;
mine is made of purpleheart and ash,
glued and peened, the iron ground

to match the sole so when to the wood
it goes, it curls bright ribbons of cedar
or larch and begins to leave a hollow

where it was, whatever shape the frame
suggests. I make the shape. I do the work.
I hit the plane on its nose or heel,

a quick clock from the mallet.
One side makes the blade
dig deeper in the wood.

The other draws it up again. I do
the work. Tap here. Tap there.
The blade is sharp;

I know how very close I am.

II

BAD YEAR ANTHEM

/////////////////////////////////////

Who can face the sea and not inherit its loneliness?

—Olin Ivory

I.

Gray sky, gray sea—*gray mind*, the man thinks. He thinks:
To grow old with it and kicks a stone into the water.

He mucks at the seam, and it crumbles below him.

A seagull beaks a crab, flights vertically and drops
it to the rocks. The man cracks with laughter,

tossing a stone to a stone.

II.

Working alone means the voice must grow louder,
for who can stand to think quietly all through the day's calculations.

I cannot. I let the voice grow loud. I let the voice
hum outside my body in distinguishable phrasings, and count

the increments as I set the fence according to the blade. All day
I stand before a blade and push things into its path.

I stand aside as what is removed is whisked alongside me.
The smallest particles of what is removed thicken the air,

making a dream inside which one cannot live. All day
the voice is learning how to be outside of the body.

III.

A man is not a beach, nor is he stone, though he collects their entirety
in a single thought. He works alone and his thoughts begin to
smack of stone. His teeth clatter with their collection.

IV.

A man can hold a secret between his teeth,
and it will never leave his mouth, for who would listen
to his wavering tune of so sad and how hard and hear

anything original? He is that he is—the errand and the fool

running to himself over and over only to find that even he
is tired of telling about it. To grow old with it

was the task, and the question always: Would he last?

A man can believe in the body and have no one,

as though he were ghost
or stone, nothing to speak at or be heard from.

V.

All work, no pay makes a body bray.
Though he may bray—

though he may bray and bray,

forgive him the bit. If he tells you his secret,
he will have no secret.

This is how one sings a sentence into stone.

REPRISE

You thought it took something special to be the hammer,
to be just right for the job, stubborn and precise
or imprecise and stubborn, at least harder than the things

you're aimed for, and heavy, as though some great
thought were kept inside your head, or at least one
long future of plinking metal or knocking wood,

for both come as naturally, which says nothing about
your claws, for to undo is as much of what you are
made for as your first assumed purpose, yet even this

says nothing of your desire—to be picked up, put to use,
to feel important to the hand that holds you, the hand
that feels like love must feel, the hand you wear as though

it were yours to claim, the sweat it works into you,
the grit, spit in the palms love, work harder love,
hit it again for the shit's gone wrong love, and no name

can make you want it more, that silver head shining
up at you like all you never had, like the man who knows
what he must finish and never puts you back.

THE HANDSHAKE

///////////////////////////////

God damn my hands
and the inward ache
that is the echo of every

hammer swing; God
damn every struck thing
and the impulse to make.

God damn the scars
and the memories they bear,
the fists I carry with me

everywhere; God damn
all that my hands fail
to hold and all they hold

too hard. I read
into the lines of each palm,
I spit into each palm, I work

each palm against each palm—
I hold my face between
my two best tools and am

ashamed. I remember
my father's father. I consider
the road. My handshake

will not tell you
what kind of man I am.

WHO BELONGS

//////////////////////////////

to the long on
& on of the boatyard's dim

cycle: boats hauled

to the tune of gravity's rude
tests, while the gravel palls

below what's left of too many

spent hulls
once ready for squalls,

now no more than

a few dark feet gone
from life's longest run:

rot's oblivion:

IN THE YEAR OF NO WORK

I would drive the pre-dawn dark to stake
my spot to fish for dinner, to numb my hands in the ice
bucket, to pluck, from the neat stack, a herring,
to fit the skullcap and pierce the eye with a toothpick,
the body double-hooked, my fingertips glimmering
with the scales of the dead while the line whined free
from the reel, and the bait arced out over the tidal current
on a point in view of the town where I lived,

where I had become a man
                                        with no money,
suddenly concerned only with money, for there were mouths
and I had helped to make them—

the eddy swirled, kept my line taut, my
whole body taut while a man a few down the row
laughed and, sitting back on his bucket, pulled in more fish
than he could take.

I hated the other men, hated the ones who caught nothing,
who crossed lines or hooked gulls, who plucked even *birds* from the sky
and slowly drew them in while they struggled, even,
finally, in the hands of the man who only wanted them free.

I climbed the breakwater and fished and spoke to no one.

I baited my line and thought of a woman
who would carry my body over the threshold
of our small white house simply with her eyes
because I had brought something home,
for her, for us, our boys at my side
while one fish was divided and indeed did feed many—

(now to sift the facts for truth):

I reeked of the sea and had nothing to show for it.

Darkling saltwater for a dream
and no other place to be.

I HAVE NO EMPIRE

to offer you,
my son, only the song

a fool travels with, on the back
of the wrong thought.

Forego the knife
in the pocket for a stone.

The only protection
from the inevitable

is patience. What better
teacher than stone?

Carry the weight well
and you'll hardly notice

how much the road
agrees with each step.

Son, the world erupts
and so grows.

When it cools,
and trust me, it does,

the crust is a tomb to living,
though the dead call it *womb*.

YOU WANT ME TO SAY IT PRETTY

but under the poison I was committed to
I can only remember the first five minutes
were so beautiful that it seems impossible

how nearly I lost my own children
to the woman who was willing to leave me

she couldn't hear the song
I made a music I sang to the feeling I sang
to who it was I thought I was and I heard it

it was an under-the-water-kind-of-song
and the house was filling with water

and the children were fish or so it seemed
but in the morning I could see I was only
asking that they hold their breath that

if they could just hold their breath a little longer
they might become fish and how lovely

to live in a house swimming with light every
prayer slurred so what it was beautiful to me
to cripple the intellect I would say to myself I

was committed to it I hardly noticed how close
I was between not wanting to live and not

knowing how to leave I was that weak
the poison that strong I wanted it to end
but I did not dare bow out

THE IMPORTANCE OF DOING NOTHING

///

It may be that when we no longer know what to do
we have come to our real work...
— Wendell Berry

When my planes squat under a film of the last month's work, I know
I will probably have to sharpen a few irons before they are once again useful to me.

And yet, I grow old at the thought of pulling the stone from the siltwater bucket.

The lever caps love their work of keeping things together and I hate to leave them
in the doldrums of the empty bench as from the frogs I slip the irons free.

I can already feel the stone's resistance as I work the first pass along the coarser face.

How thin must a workable edge be? One must be unable to see even the slightest
glare at the blade's very tip.

I have made so many mistakes.

FROM THE MIDDLE OF IT

Out here on Discovery in the songlight

of another long day walking sheets

through the blade and drawing shapes

upon the bare walls of the house

my children will someday return to

as strangers and maybe for a moment

remember the summer I worked

like a madman, the land and the house so new

to them every turn was a revelation,

and the well dried up and the cats

each day tossed field mice in small arcs

above the grass like confetti while the boys

tore through the yard on a rush of home-

picked berries, feral almost they were

in their joy, every cut close to the bone—

the days of one step forward, four steps back,

stumbling about with the clatter

of hammers and blades, wondering

over clearances and systems, seeing visions

of plumbed lines behind walls

tapping out a slow leak, or a dream

of whatever rot there was

already written into the story of the house;

what it was to want to own and then to wear

the worry of ownership, to wear and try

to shuck it off to chase the boys

around the lawn only to find my father's voice

coming from my mouth directing

them through tasks with the same measured

calmness that wore me thin when he spoke,

and even as I was returned to myself

I could see no other way to be

and so focused on the small joys:

opening the faucet slowly to the sweet

run of water filling a glass, imagining

the aquifer below us, the well, the pump,

the passageways through which the water

travels, through which it will

continue to pass, and in those moments

I spoke the final words of a poem:

nothing in this world is ours

as we strolled through the mossy paths

of our woods, *nothing in this world is ours*

to the broken toy, to the broken tool,

to the dead mouse, the dead rabbit, *nothing*

in this world is ours to the wasted food,

to the hole in the wall, to the wall itself,

nothing in this world is ours whispered

to my boys, my wife asleep in the loft,

my hands passing over the unfinished

work, as I wondered how it would feel

looking back over and over my own flaws

as I made my way through the years,

even the smallest of errors apparent—

I stood there at my life and touched

the edges and wanted to love everything,

even the time it took to get here,

and for a brief moment felt exactly

what I knew I would never have.

SONG OF TOMORROW

Now I begin with the hands of my two sons,
clutching the small predictions for their lives with what

every father knows, each digit soft and already
damaged—I cannot save them—these two bright

chances at my side, burning blonde in the sun,
singing at every sweetness, berries, ripe, or not,

torn from the bush; they hardly whimper
for my help, knowing, *believing*, I will give

them whatever I have, whatever I can acquire, and so,
what I mean to acquire is a kindness beyond me, my means

a willingness to dig myself in, to surround myself
with to-do-lust, and do the most happening things

with our time; I am a man trying
to hold water in cupped hands—I will fail

to hold it; I will fail, but I will know
what joy there is in feeling it pass.

III

CENTER OF EFFORT

Though you may not hear these words,
they belong to the boat, or the boat
to them: *gooseneck, throat nock, topping
lift, parrel,* and the traveler runs slick
along the horse, helps the mainsheet
stay trim, which means full, which
means movement, the line locked
in the jaws of the cleat, and the cant
of the boat reminds you of a particular
man you knew as a child—was he your
teacher?—who always cocked his head
to one side while talking to you
as if everything were a question, were
a curiosity to be considered
from a fresh angle, and the boat
looks at you the same way, until
the only answer can be wind, which
never tells you what it means, but
often sounds like yes.

O ANCHOR
////////////////////

Dark charms the anchor in its house

of water and what type of bottom
does it drag, for what type of work, for you,

with your need to stay in roughly the same place

for a night, with your questions of how
much to let out

and how well your windlass works

and how you feel sometimes hauling
200 foot of chain by hand in the dark,

wondering what in your life sent you

here, where the world exists as much
below you as above; where you are

as much the chain as the chain.

NOCTURNE WITH MYSTERIOUS LEAK

Water's running down the wall
to the floorboards, making

a bad stain, a warping of the wood, a rotting—

and the white paint is growing fat with water,
brown runs like banks of a distant river, no depth

to the run, so it's like a map of what's happened.

Everything has been pushed to the middle of the room
like a raft of upholstery in a pond of wood.

A lamp flickers and goes out. A pale light creeps

through the glass, and you climb onto the raft and listen
to the patter grow to a heavy hushing, a song of *nothing*

can be done and so you do nothing,

just captain the couch flotilla, drifting off,
charting the flooded country of

this room named for the living.

IN THE BOATYARD

I.

there lives a weather vane   copper salt-green

pitched roof   above the racking hull

rafters & scaffolding   dirt floor under floor

of every shaving yet made from the work

II.

the men oiled   worked   to a sheen in their heavy clothes

tattered as the wind   as the wind worked

over the dusty yard and who

was there to claim such derelict caskets   propped upon

III.

jack stands   stripped and abandoned

with every kind of name for hope   or luck   or pleasure

lettered darkly on each transom

AND
////////

Flies wake themselves from the end we believe we've witnessed

and buzz winter out of their bone. They live again

and for what? To blink against the window over

and over, the tirade of their want a reminder of what lives in me

and, therefore, my son, in you. This glissando ligature that belongs to the mouth

and the ear. But more so to water, for it is all

and. Perhaps that is why we bathe in it. To feel carried on the backs of ghosts

and gods. To feel how gently it lifts

and drowns, while something in us wakes

and, to the glass we do not know is there, takes us full force onward, glistening
   with hum

and furthermore.

ODE TO THE PREACHER JIG

To make the makeshift
jig, one must only reach

into the box
                        below

the bandsaw's bed, plates
of doorskin scrap

and cedar wedges, mahogany
this and that's for some odd

job on nearly any day. Simple as it is
amazing, that from this waste a tool

for working blindly and precise
might rise in crude form,

flaking at its edges, true only
at its corresponding points,

where passes no divine
correspondence, yet

a chosen version
of the world: *Keep this,*

cut that. And the rest of the story
belongs to the wood.

FOR THE NEXT TASK, I TURN
FROM THE BENCH

with one hundred bronze clench nails

in a wide mouth mason, the bucking iron's
finger gap smooth upon my hand,

the hammer longing for its sway, to meet

each nail's head gently, to send the slender
tooth into its bread, whereupon the head

is backed by weighted hand, that the tapered

spike may be driven in reverse, the soft-tapping
slow dance of the working bend,

that the golden nail may re-enter

the wood from which it came, & holdfast
two strakes together, that the many

may share a single name.

[AND NOW THE SONG OF A MAN]

And now the song of a man

who has been to the sawyer,
his oiled mill tuned

to the wants of the work,
each filed tooth of bandsaw's

looped blade gleaning
into the tree's unseen, whereby

the wanted shape is laid bare,
and the maker no more must make.

THE MAGAZINE

is evening-lit in your hands
so the boat it shows

in its small square of water
has the light of the room, the windows

behind you, the reflected bay—
the magazine's horizon

nearly the same, so no matter
how you try to strip the room

of metaphor and meaning, the room
becomes the boat, which you are in,

hardly alone with your red sails
and curtain wind

I WEAR THE WORK UPON MY CLOTHES

To enter the shop is to enter the acolyte's chamber
and I take the table saw as seriously as god,
and know that inside every roughsawn plank there lives
some version of the devil, a deviation

from the path laid out boldly on the board,
the pencil's dark pressed deep into the grain
such that a small channel has been crushed
into the wood, a reminder to live as closely

to the truth as one is able, even
though truth is what will take your fingers,
or send slivers deep into your hands.
When I come home after it all,

and strip down to my thinnest self, my clothes, they
do not forget; they wait and wait on the hook
that holds them; I walk away
and still they keep my shape.

BALLAST

///////////////////

Many years I held the list
of a sailboat as my greatest fear
for it seemed I was always
about to spill over one edge
of myself into another version
of what I could not say, for I
had no idea what it was
that held me fast to the earth,
and my knowledge of the small
boat's underside was clear:
nothing there but the slit
through which a dagger board
could slide. I had maybe half
an idea of how the leaning
put the weight of the water
on our side, but many times,
in small lakes, I had gone over
and found myself once more
still alive, even in the middle
of my fear, but the larger
boats I've learned to love
had more need than a single
board could answer, for the cant
could make a monster
of a boat's fair lines were it not
for a small mountain of mined
lead poured into the shape
of the architect's design,
blocked and bolted through to
the backbone's wooden members
that under way she could
dip her rails and keep

a friendship with this movement,
so that now I might say a love
has grown in me
for the impossibly heavy.

I HAVE A CANVAS WORK TOTE ENTIRELY DEVOTED

to my essential hammers, and all my hammers
are essential, each mallet, sledge, cross- and ball-peen,

bronze-headed, shafts of angular hickory

or smoothed ash, a few worn to the thin edge
of their lives by the work of strangers who

abandoned them to thrift, their heads clamoring

together in the bag's soot-dark, while, as in the marina's
masted haven, their handles rise up past

the canvas horizon, begging to be used.

MAKING A RABBET PLANE IN THE MACHINE SHOP ON THE HILL

I fish for angle iron in the scrap,
slag clotted along the seams
of all but one piece clean enough
to make it worth the work ahead.
I lock it in the vice, jaws closed
down with the rubber mallet's
prodding, and the grinder whines on
in my hands, works the rusted
metal to a sheen, swirling Q's
left in wake until I take the piece
to the belt and let the rough tongue
lick it smooth. The whole
room smells hot; it
smells of origin, of soot, and
the bandsaw screeches as the blade
sinks through. The shape
I want is marked on the metal
and what I can't take out quickly
and with power must be worked
by hand. A rattail file finds
the mouth of the almost-plane
and works a bevel smooth. The blade
is an old file I've ground the teeth
off of. I give it an edge
and it stays. It gives me an edge,
the smell of the metal shop,
a cutting bitter scent that belongs
inside the earth. I turn
the idea of the tool over in my hands.

That it works makes me want to work.
The work, it carves that want away.

ODE TO THE SLICK

Half of the tool is heft, its weight
given to the single-minded
& shining, to the thinnest want

for cutting, ground hollow & honed,
this tooth made for to enter
the skin of the wood, for to lessen

the body of what it is; in one's hands,
it asks to be put to task, it cleaves
to the wood, raising long strips of what is

there—it: ancient; it: your grandfather's
grandfather; it: the bone
of a man who could make anything,

the making-bone, we shall call it,
that even in its hunger can, with grace,
lift translucent scarfs from

the heaviest of timbers, through which
one can clearly see the world.

BEFORE THE BOAT IS A BOAT

it is constellation, is
gridwork, a pencil-line frame

on the floor, points nailed
into doorskin around which a batten

is wrapped, around which the eye
also bends, until the line is made fair,

which means *sweet*, which means *true*,
which means the eye

is still the most right tool.
All this from numbers alone,

measurements to be drawn
in four perspectives, but not so darkly,

as any star can be wrong, yet still
righted, this work of nails and arcs

from which the boat rises,
its pencil sheer and tumblehome,

the architecture of the backbone—everything
erased at least once, every line redrawn.

END GRAIN

////////////////////

is an opening, is all
we can see

of the long
strands that make

the pathways for
rays, bisecting

annular rings,
the most

vulnerable door
of what makes

the holiest of
things.

IT'S THE BOAT THAT HAUNTS YOU

And so it is, the boat has come to own you,
has learned to speak a language you cannot help

but agree with, its voice the dark lapping
of water against the hull, its song the wind

in the stays while you sleep, dreaming of a bowsprit
to hold you against the waves, and the boat

curls golden bracelets of cedar
around your wrists as you plane each

plank, its touch the dream of a body becoming
whole—to make the shape, to be shaped—and the boat

says, *Please,* says, *The honed edge*
against clear grain is my small prayer to your devotion.

May you forget your life, may you
always be close.

HOUSE OF WATER

If, when in the house of water, you do not
somehow feel both kept and free
you are no kin to me.

My kin worry of the drain, but let
the faucet drip. We hear a voice
that is both young and old in it.

My kin, we work to house the water
yet know we cannot keep anything
but the ache of sweet *was*—

how soon that song is learned
still amazes me. I heard it from my boy,
red and wet in my arms, still corded

to the womb. The melody was in
the afterbirth still lifting waves
across that membrane's silver skin.

It kept on in hum until the boy
had drunk up all the notes. My kin, we live
to know the hurt of what we cannot keep.

There is a memory in the water,
a name we ache to hear, though to say it
takes no sound. There is no sound

we can make, but to be the well,
the welling, the walls and what is walled in,
so close to one's self one can almost see

under this body's skin, the sea.

NOTES

"Ode to the Steam Box"
    The steam box is used for bending frames, stems, and planks in
    traditional boatbuilding.

"Ode to the Gain"
    Gain (n)—a bevel cut into plank ends in traditional lapstrake boat
    construction that allows otherwise lapped planks to lay flush at stem
    and transom.

"Backing Out"
    A backing out plane is a specialty tool often used in planking and oar
    making.

"From the Middle of It" takes a line from Joshua Poteat's
    "Nocturne: For the Aviaries."

"Ode to the Preacher Jig"
    A preacher is a custom-made boatbuilder's tool which allows one to
    transfer an accurate cutline from one face of a board to the other.

"Ode to the Slick"
    Slick (n)—a large chisel used mainly by shipwrights and timber framers.

BOOK BENEFACTORS

//////////////////////////

Alice James Books wishes to thank the following individual(s) who generously contributed toward the publication of *House of Water:*

Rebecca Brown-Nienow
Delaney Dechant

For more information about AJB's book benefactor program, contact us via phone or email, or visit alicejamesbooks.org to see a list of forthcoming titles.

RECENT TITLES FROM ALICE JAMES BOOKS

Alice James Books has been publishing poetry since 1973. The press was founded in Boston, Massachusetts as a cooperative wherein authors performed the day-to-day undertakings of the press. This collaborative element remains viable even today, as authors who publish with the press are also invited to become members of the editorial board and participate in editorial decisions at the press. The editorial board selects manuscripts for publication via the press's annual, national competition, the Alice James Award. Alice James Books seeks to support women writers and was named for Alice James, sister to William and Henry, whose extraordinary gift for writing went unrecognized during her lifetime.

Designed by Anna Reich
Anna Reich Design | anna@annareichdesign.com

Printed by McNaughton & Gunn